First World War
and Army of Occupation
War Diary
France, Belgium and Germany

32 DIVISION
96 Infantry Brigade,
Brigade Trench Mortar Battery
1 August 1916 - 31 August 1916

WO95/2398/3

The Naval & Military Press Ltd
www.nmarchive.com
Published in association with The National Archives

Published by

The Naval & Military Press Ltd

Unit 10 Ridgewood Industrial Park,
Uckfield, East Sussex,
TN22 5QE England
Tel: +44 (0) 1825 749494

www.naval-military-press.com
www.nmarchive.com

This diary has been reprinted in facsimile from the original. Any imperfections are inevitably reproduced and the quality may fall short of modern type and cartographic standards.

© **Crown Copyright**
Images reproduced by permission of The National Archives, London, England, 2015.

Contents

Document type	Place/Title	Date From	Date To
Heading	WO95/2398/3		
Heading	32nd Division 96th Infy Bde 96th Trench Mortar Bty Aug 1916		
Heading	96th Brigade. 32nd Division. 96th Trench Mortar Battery August 1916		
Heading	War Diary 96th Trench Mortar Battery For The Month Of August 1916. Vol 1		
War Diary	Ruitz	01/08/1916	04/08/1916
War Diary	Bethune	05/08/1916	21/08/1916
War Diary	Cambron Sector	22/08/1916	22/08/1916
War Diary	Trenches. Cambrin Sector	23/08/1916	26/08/1916
War Diary	Cambrin Sector	26/08/1916	31/08/1916

WO 95/2398/3

32ND DIVISION
96TH INFY BDE

96TH TRENCH MORTAR BTY
AUG 1916

96th Brigade.
32nd Division.

96th TRENCH MORTAR BATTERY

AUGUST 1 9 1 6

Army Form C. 2118

Vol 1

WAR DIARY
or
INTELLIGENCE SUMMARY

(Erase heading not required.)

Confidential

War Diary 96th French Motor Battery
for the month of August 1916.

H Sergman 2 Lt
9 LT M/3

Army Form C. 2118.

WAR DIARY
or
INTELLIGENCE SUMMARY
(Erase heading not required.)

Instructions regarding War Diaries and Intelligence Summaries are contained in F. S. Regs., Part II. and the Staff Manual respectively. Title Pages will be prepared in manuscript.

Place	Date	Hour	Summary of Events and Information	Remarks and references to Appendices
Ruitz	1.8.16		Battery Training — Running, Physical Training, Rifle Exercises and Gun Drill	
Ruitz	2.8.16		Battery Training — Running, Physical Training, Gun Drill and Bombing	
Ruitz	3.8.16		Battery Training — Running, Physical Training, Bombing, Rifle Exercises	
Ruitz	4.8.16		Battery Training — Running, Physical Training, Gun Drill, Bombing	
BETHUNE	5.8.16		Moved to this place	
BETHUNE	6.8.16		Church Parade in Grande Place for celebration of 2nd Anniversary of Address by Gen Sir C Munro K.M.G. K.C.B. GOC 1st Army & M.G. K.C.B. GOC 1st Army & Sir C Munro C Munro Castleton C Munro	

2449 Wt. W14957/M90 750,000 1/16 J.B.C. & A. Forms/C.2118/12.

WAR DIARY
or
INTELLIGENCE SUMMARY

Army Form C. 2118

(Erase heading not required.)

Place	Date	Hour	Summary of Events and Information	Remarks and references to Appendices
BÉTHUNE	8.16		~~Parade of Battery~~. Battery Training. Running, Physical Training, Bombing, Gun Drill	
BÉTHUNE	8.8.16		Route March of about 10 miles	
BÉTHUNE	9.8.16		Battery Training. Running, Bombing, Gun Drill	
BÉTHUNE	10.8.16		Battery Training. Running, Gun Drill, Rifle Exercises, Bayonet Fighting. Visited by Divisional General; Major General W.H. Rycroft CB, CMG	
BÉTHUNE	11.8.16		Battery Training. Live Bomb Throwing, Gun Drill. Bayonet Fighting	
BÉTHUNE	12.8.16		Battery Training. Gun Drill (Tactical Work), Bayonet Fighting, Cleaning Guns	
BÉTHUNE	13.8.16		Church Parade for Battery. 2 Officers + SNCO's visited trenches at Cambrin sector preparatory to taking over same.	

Army Form C. 2118.

WAR DIARY
or
INTELLIGENCE SUMMARY
(*Erase heading not required.*)

Instructions regarding War Diaries and Intelligence Summaries are contained in F. S. Regs., Part II. and the Staff Manual respectively. Title Pages will be prepared in manuscript.

Place	Date	Hour	Summary of Events and Information	Remarks and references to Appendices
BÉTHUNE	14.8.16		Battery Gunnery. Physical Training, Bayonet fighting, Bombing &c	
BÉTHUNE	15.8.16		Inspection of Battery by S.O.C. 96th Brigade. Suggestions received and acted upon. The open order.	
BÉTHUNE	16.8.16		Inspection of Battery by S.O.C. 96th Brigade. Suggestions of previous day acted upon. Physical Drill & Bayonet fighting	
BÉTHUNE	17.8.16		Battery Training. Physical Training, Bombing, Bayonet fighting, Rifle Exercises	
BÉTHUNE	18.8.16		Battery Training. Physical Training, Bayonet fighting also Kit Inspection.	
BÉTHUNE	19.8.16		Battery Training. Physical Training & Bayonet fighting. Rain interfered with further work in the open.	
BÉTHUNE	20.8.16		Church Parade.	

WAR DIARY
or
INTELLIGENCE SUMMARY
(Erase heading not required.)

Army Form C. 2118.

Place	Date	Hour	Summary of Events and Information	Remarks and references to Appendices
BÉTHUNE	21.8.16	4.30 a.m.	Left BÉTHUNE for trenches in the Cambrin Sector. 4 Guns in the line at points A.27.b.20.90, A.27.d.80.60, A.27.d.90.60, A.28.c.30.20. It is proposed to increase this number to 6 as soon as emplacements can be built for the extra 2 guns. The afternoon was quiet, but at 6 o'clock the enemy sent over occasional rifle-grenades and oil-cans. The guns at A.27.d.80.60 and A.27.d.90.60 replied vigorously and the oil cans ceased though the rifle grenades continued for some little time afterwards.	
Cambrin Sector	22.8.16		In the morning when the gun at A.27.b.20.90, was registering at A.27.b.80.90, sniper reported that shell droppings fairly working in the trenches. At 3 in the afternoon, all 4 guns replied vigorously to enemy's retaliation for bombardment in the Cuinchy Sector. Quiet the rest of the day.	

WAR DIARY
or
INTELLIGENCE SUMMARY

Army Form C. 2118.

Place	Date	Hour	Summary of Events and Information	Remarks and references to Appendices
Trenches Cambrin Sector	23.8.16	3 pm	Retaliation to enemy's rifle grenades between fronts	
		5 pm	Retaliation to enemy's oil-cans, rifle grenades between A 26 a 10.10. and A 28 c 60.60. Retaliation at 9 o'clock to enemy's rifle-grenades when same was exploded. Rest of night quiet.	
do.	24.8.16	3 pm	Retaliation for oil cans and rifle grenades.	
		11.40 pm	Organised bombardment of enemy's front line between fronts A 28 c 40. 45" and A 28 a 03. One of guns received a direct hit on top of emplacement, but owing to good roof, neither team nor gun were damaged.	
do.	25.8.16	1.15 am	Fire slackened. Rest of night and morning quiet. Evening enemy sent over a number of rifle grenades to which Stokes replied vigorously. On the explosion of the mine in the left sector, we successfully were down retaliation of enemy's rifle-grenades, whiz-bangs etc. Rest of night quiet.	
do.	26.8.16	12.30 pm	Enemy fired numerous rifle grenades for 5 minutes. We retaliated	

WAR DIARY
or
INTELLIGENCE SUMMARY

(Erase heading not required.)

Army Form C. 2118.

Place	Date	Hour	Summary of Events and Information	Remarks and references to Appendices
Canbrem Linkor	26.8.16		About 3 p.m. the enemy sent over salvos of whizz-bangs. to which we retaliated	
do	27.8.16		Stokes 3" Mortars. replied to enemy's bombardment of rum jars and whizz-bangs.	
		6.30am		
		8.0am	The afternoon of the 27 was quiet until about 4.30 pm when enemy heavily bombarded our left sub-sector with rifle-grenades and whizz-bangs. Stokes Mortars bombarded enemy's front line and kept down rifle-grenade fire.	
do	28.8.16	4.15 pm	Heavy Artillery bombarded enemy's lines about Railway Point A.28.c.2.1. Stokes Mortars took Part in the bombardment The two guns firing between A.28.a.1.1 & A.28.c.5.5 fired very successfully about 90 rounds.	
do	29.8.16		Morning Quiet. Co Battalions were being relieved, we refrained	

Army Form C. 2118

WAR DIARY
or
INTELLIGENCE SUMMARY

(Erase heading not required.)

Instructions regarding War Diaries and Intelligence Summaries are contained in F. S. Regs., Part II. and the Staff Manual respectively. Title Pages will be prepared in manuscript.

Place	Date	Hour	Summary of Events and Information	Remarks and references to Appendices
Cambrin Sector	29.8.16		from mutual retaliation.	
Cambrin Sector	30.8.16		Quiet along the whole of the line owing to working parties being out repairing after storm. Retaliation by enemy was mostly by rifle-grenades.	
Cambrin Sector	31.8.16		Morning very quiet.	

1875 Wt. W593/826 1,000,000 4/15 J.B.C. & A. A.D.S.S./Forms/C. 2118.

www.ingramcontent.com/pod-product-compliance
Lightning Source LLC
Chambersburg PA
CBHW081254170426
43191CB00037B/2152